TO THE HEART OF THINGS

Mark Howitt

AUGUR PRESS

TO THE HEART OF THINGS

Copyright © Mark Howitt 2019

The moral right of the author has been asserted

British Library Cataloguing in Publication Data.
A catalogue record for this book is available from
the British Library.

ISBN 978-1-911229-05-6

First published 2019 by
Augur Press
Delf House
52 Penicuik Road
Roslin
Midlothian EH25 9LH
United Kingdom

TO THE HEART OF THINGS

Dedication:

To God, from whence my gift came.

To my mother, family and friends who have supported me through my troubles. And to everyone who inspired my poems and those who encouraged me towards publication.

Contents

On Poetry

Have you noticed how it is
When writing poetry
That my ideas are never his,
He disagrees with me?

The words I choose most never rhyme
If chosen for their sense,
And verbs when right are all the time
Made senseless by their tense.

When tense and rhyme and most of all
Their meaning are all fine,
Then scansion comes and proves my fall,
And ruins verse and line.

So why do I write poetry,
Why don't I stick to prose?
Perhaps it's something born in me
That loves it, but who knows?

Introduction

Mark Howitt has recently returned to writing poetry after a long fallow period. He started writing in his teens and continued through university years. After that he wrote very little for about 30 years. Then an internal dam burst and poetry has flowed from him ever since.

Much of Mark's poetry is meticulously crafted in a variety of classical forms of metre, structure and style. Although maintaining such forms, he is never satisfied unless the poem flows in both words and sense: in words, so that the reading or recital is smooth and un-laboured; in sense, so that the structure supports the development of the poem in its exploration of the subject. In this way, while walking in the shadows of the great classical poets, he seeks to make his poems manifestations of a particular kind of beauty.

For subject matter Mark mainly chooses the world around him, and his deep faith. Some poems dwell on surface beauty, but most delve into the soul and spirit of the subject, or into reflections on how things of nature can be allegories of profound realities.

Unusually for a poet, Mark has no literary background: he is a scientist, technologist and entrepreneur. Most weekends he loves to walk in the hills and mountains, and usually composes his poetry on such walks. His love of nature shines through many of his poems, and his love of people through most of the rest as he seeks to understand their motivations and compassionately lays bare their souls.

While a number of Mark's poems have been published in newspapers and magazines of limited circulation, this is his first published selection.

The Bridge

Helping the trav'lers of life's rocky flow,
Easing the way across hazards and streams,
Trodden and trampled, scarce noticed below
By practical people and dreamers of dreams.

Some try to cross with huge burdens and train,
Saying I should be demolished, replaced,
Bypassed, neglected, avoided, disdained:
My purpose surpassed, my presence misplaced.

My shame is to block an inadequate way;
My misery, insults abusive and snide;
My sadness, neglect, or be bypassed around.

To shorten and smooth paths I stand and I lay,
My pleasure to help, to keep safe and to guide,
My joy to assist where life's journeys are bound.

The Bramble Patch

The bramble patch within the garden thrives
Un-tackled, still encroaching wide and free,
So thickly choking flowers, lawns, and trees:
Invading alien swallowing light and lives.

I cut it back to keep it in its place,
Yet still the tangle thickens, blossoms, spreads.
I reach to prune still further from the beds –
Much slower, scratching, harder work to face.

So must I grasp and tug and pull
To grub it out, then digging make a cull.
The tiring painful progress takes its toll
Yet sole this slog removes the cancer full.

You pray that I should help and do my part:
Say how should I approach your brambled heart?

The Substitute

Born
Into a home
Divided,
Unloved and alone,
Shaken by quarrels, torn by strife,
The fragile shell that surrounded his life
So cold and uncaring,
Not shared with, not sharing,
Derided
His substitute for a home.

Sent
Into a school
Impersonal.
Conformed to a rule
Enforced and yet not understood;
An education so he could
Conform to society
In all its propriety.
He found futile
This substitute for knowledge.

Grew
In search of ideals,
Rejecting
What so well conceals
The truth that must give life meaning;
The world's façade falls revealing
Its shallow duplicity,
Its seeming futility
Reflecting
His substitute for a youth.

Loved
And loving her too
So dearly
That it could last through
A lifetime in each other's heart.
They swore that they would never part.
Together they slept
Soon after she left,
Showing clearly
His substitute for love.

Worked
A life on the move
And hard working.
So as to improve
His comfort and his social ease –
More money, more worry, more needs –
Until he retires
Against his desires,
Remembering
His substitute for life.

Died.
His children stay,
His mourning wife –
They seem to say
His life fulfilled has left with them
A great example for all men.
Death has shaved him bare
Of all, yet none there
Sees through his life
A substitute for death.

How
Did he not know
Reality?
How did he grow
To life, whose work is death, not gleaning
A man once came and gave life meaning?
Him we crucified;
He gave us when he died
Totality
Of fullness for our lives.

Unequal to the Struggle?

Civilian caught to fight in global war,
Untrained, unequal to our foe before,
My narrow mind and home-bound soul and heart
Not comprehending even my small part.

Struggling hard, how can I see the flow
Of battle; how can I the whole war know?
Fatigue and wounds, despair and doubt in force,
One step from falling, how to trust our course?

Yet faith believes, sustains me through the fight;
And hope still pierces darkness with its light.
A purpose love provides amid encircling wrong,
And truth my weapon always sharp and strong.
While oft eclipsed by worry, failure, pain,
My unseen God will always me sustain.

Vengeance

O man, why can you not behold
Yourself with true, unblinkered sight,
And see the fraud in what is told
Of human goodness, love and might?

Unveil your eyes, O man, and see
Your poison touch, redoubled lies,
The seething broth of misery
Created by your cursèd eyes.

Why see you not must sometime end
This cycle of ascending woes;
That evil on itself must bend,
How soon we reap what mankind sows?

The guiltless blood cries from the ground
A plea for vengeance on this world,
Entreaties echoing around;
Their vindication is unfurled.

Yet who the hearer, whose reply?
Who hears with power through the grave?
How can you fight, or even try,
A foe unknown with unknown ways?

A foe unknown, O man, to you,
Yet known by some, to them a friend,
Whose way is sure, whose love is true,
Who vengeance will with justice send.

After the Battle

He wiped his dripping sword and stood there, a lone black figure, while his men trod slowly towards their sombre horses. He stayed, frozen by his sadness, petrified by the sullen silence, empty despite a sense of sinking in the depths of his crying heart. There had been life, happy life, where now there was death – inescapable death, all-enveloping death, silent death, joyless death, death. And he had brought this death; he had *become* death, he *was* death. Death for a cause lost before it came into being, lost and hopeless.

Aftermath

No tree on its roots, no beast on its feet,
No animals live, no bark, cry nor bleat.
No light in the sky, no sun's radiant heat;
The cold dark of day turned windless night.

The rivers so dry, the grass plains so bare,
The pools of no water, the stifling air.
Not even a vulture in death's newest lair;
The silence so loud, the darkness of light.

The flocks of dead birds haunting the air,
The living remains of carrion there.
The huge grazing herds of animals slain
Watching for hunters to death long since lain.
The desolate plain of lately ceased strife
Proclaiming with silence that death has new life.

Piercing through his darkest thoughts he heard a baby crying. He began to walk slowly towards that cry. The mother peered covertly out of the tent. He sensed that she had the baby in her arms.

She saw the black-clad man walking towards her. She had seen him before, in his state of raging fury, slashing right and left, killing all who came near, and now he was approaching *her*. Yet his eyes were not flaming now as they had been then; they had no malice or madness in them and he was sheathing his stained sword. So she did not flee, but stood, clutching her weeping infant to her breast, eyeing the man.

He came close, held out his hands and gently took the baby, who fell silent. He looked up, and his gaze fixed on the battlefield beyond the woman. She saw great sadness in his eyes, a sadness tinged with despair, and she knew the void within him.

Then he looked down at the baby and seemed to contemplate it for a while before raising his eyes back to the field of death. Standing motionless, his eyes revealed his soul as tears ran slowly down his cheeks.

The woman saw in his eyes a sadness that seemed to stretch from a bottomless gulf in his past and reach through to the future.

As she watched, once more he looked down at the baby in his arms, and his face softened. The despair slowly left his eyes and a tinge of joy dawned in his mourning soul.

A vision of the freedom for which he was fighting shone through the darkness in his mind.

The Vision of Freedom

Through numbing sorrow of his mind
A vision rose, still undefined,
Of light and joy in all mankind
With hopeless darkness left behind;

Of widest streets with great crowds filled,
The crowds whose dreams had been fulfilled,
Their weed-grown fields of joy now tilled,
The fears of living newly stilled;

Of cheering, shouting, joyous throngs,
Enraptured music, hymns and songs,
Of laughter ringing all night long;
Suppression now a nightmare gone.

His vision went and now he saw
The hopeless darkness him before,
The evils that were lain in store,
His goal, the ending of this war.

His men had ridden slowly up to him. He gave the baby back
to its mother, glanced at the four at the head of his company,
mounted his great black steed, and rode off with them into the
deepening gloom. The dying sun fled the bloody sky, and
darkness was master of the field.

Points of View – A Stone

A stone to trip, to clear from bed and field,
To throw for harm, threaten, cause to yield.
A stone to build some steps, a wall, a home,
To sculpt and etch, to lay a cornerstone.

A rock to block, impeding there our way,
To crush, destroy, demolish, even slay.
A rock to build cathedrals, castles tall,
Commemorate the greatest of us all.

The hills, less fertile, cannot crops sustain
Or any population great contain.
The hills which earth's great ores display
And offer souls some respite from life's fray.

A mountain range resists life's ebb and flow
And progress, forcing pace of life to slow.
A mountain refuge for the wildlife fair,
To scrape the clouds of rain, the streams to bear.

The Dale in Spring

Amid the lush upholstered greens
Meander freshly placid streams
That nature's bounty careful hides
Within the valley's womb-like sides.

Dispersed within is wealth untold
In royal purple, blue and gold,
Scattered pastels daintily
With white, in starburst symmetry.

Above the orchid footings rise,
In yellow carpets to the skies,
The gorse-clad hillsides careful keep
Below the lofty pastures steep
The gentle tones and joyful ease
Of fair chromatic symphonies.

Lamaload in Autumn

The reservoir lies calm beneath the fold,
Harboured safe between its wooded banks.
The larches' needle carpet is unrolled
While autumn shades adorn its flanks.

The ancient pack-horse trail mounts the hill
Between a dry-stone wall and steep decline
To summits warmed by sun, yet windy chill
Revealing views of Cheshire's plain so fine.

On gliding breeze the quartering buzzard mews
To neighbours, startling woodland beasts and birds
While wary sheep the coming stranger view,
The squirrels leap, the rabbits flee, the sheepdog stirs.

Unmarked, the age-old track descends
In zig-zag route down hillside thickets steep
Till fording nascent river as it wends
I mount the hill mid flocks of watching sheep.

The gusting wind spits rain my neck to cool
And forms a rainbow whole in skies ahead.
The sun ducks under clouds of wispy wool
Enlivening colours, second arc to shed.

Returning as the rose-pink sunset fades,
Two lovers, happy in their lonesome way
Passed by, low chatting as the last light fades
To night's more tranquil pleasures close the day.

Bowness at Dawn

Wrapped cosily in silken mists,
Protected from the cold,
Surrounded by the gentle hills,
A town lies in a fold.

Encircled by the green clad fells
The lake rests peaceful calm;
And sleeping also on its shores
The outline of a farm.

Amid the cow and sheep-strewn fields
The twinkling streetlights seem
To be embraced as by the mists,
By small, contented dreams.

The mist seems like a dreamt-of sea,
The hills a far-off land;
The treetops float like fairy isles,
The streets a starlit strand.

Then o'er the hills in eastern sky
The sun comes clothed in gold;
And by the sound of churchyard bells
Another morning tolled.

Then slowly street-lamp stars go out,
The dream-sea disappears,
The fairy isles take root and go,
The town wakes to its years.

Observed from the ruined shepherd's hut at Scale Ivy Intakes.

The Whistling Wind

As I walked the whistling wind
Chilled and challenged up the scarp,
Tired and wint'ry daylight dimmed,
Colours washed and frosted sharp.

Shelt'ring calm in hilltop cleft,
Musing on the year expired;
Events and people, warp and weft,
Woven in long struggles tired.

Struck, assailed, besieged by all,
Some who should know better quit.
Stumbling, yet I never fall;
My soul from you was never split.

Work and family, hope and faith
Shaken utter to the core,
Yet preserved more than a wraith:
Honour, character and more.

Dying year proclaims the new
Born as from the old year's flames.
Hope eternal, vision true:
'The future's yours' the wind proclaims.

The Fallen Leaves

The fallen leaves lie littered on the bank,
Leathered brown, devoid of living green;
The trees above stand gaunt in lifeless rank,
Their once luxuriant forms now naked seen.

The pines full-clad proclaim majestic show,
Their poisoned needles near bereft of feed;
Proudly green, yet choking soil below,
A showy desert yields not even seed.

Yet look again at winter's boughs so stark:
The hints of buds bide time until the spring;
The sap flows still beneath the gnarlèd bark;
Dead leaves the very soil its feed do bring.
Among what seems alive, there none can live,
Sole that which dies each year true life can give.

Winter

Bare trees shiver in the howling wind,
Dead leaves run in frenzied search for rest,
The ice-cold rain assails the frozen ground,
Creatures left, no shelter to be found.

The trees, once friendly, turn their backs on life;
They leave the beasts deserted and alone.
Their leaves gave shelter, nuts gave food for all;
When needed most, they took that time to fall.

The grass provided grazing for all beasts –
When winter came it chose then not to grow.
The flowers gave the animals their seeds;
In autumn died, their place usurped by weeds.

The shrubs provided food and hidden nests,
Yet came the cold and they withdrew them both.
The brambles gave protection, berries, leaves;
And now they're dead, no friend 'gainst murderous foes.

Some beasts fled to burrows underground,
They search for roots to keep them safe and fed.
Nourishment nigh impossible to find,
The frozen ground now too hard to be mined.

The fearful beasts, so hungry and so cold,
They cannot feed – there is no food to find.
They cannot hide from wind nor predator;
They die by cold, by starving or by slaughter.

Crescendo

While winter fettered all the life and land
And dulled the muted green and brown of hill,
All plants and creatures hunkered to withstand
For mere survival 'gainst the winter's chill.

As winter's grip fatigues, the first spring plants
Creep tentatively from their hiding dens.
Some birds chirp quizzical demands
That spring awaken, life to start again.

Then birds' crescendo breaks, their song resounds
"There's more to life than mere survival here:
Renewal, joy and liveliness where love abounds."
The lambs respond with prancing, playful cheer;
The brightening grass, the trees' new leaves unfurled,
The plants in splendour paint the waking world.

Silence

Assailed by silence deep and long,
No laughter, voice: bereft and void
Down maelstrom swept by currents strong,
Despairing, worthless, hope devoid.

Accepting silence rests my soul
Unsatisfied by broadcast sound
To search in life's slow moving shoal
To place its feet on firmer ground.

Ent'ring silence, thinking through
My life, my loves and miseries,
A new perspective comes in view –
The tranquil water my soul frees.

Embracing silence to explore
All things with heart, with soul and mind,
New meaning in the world before,
Strong currents soft my spirit find.

The Vine's Branches

The more the branches bear on me
The stronger they will be.
The more they drink the living flow
Of sap, the greater grow.

This life could clothe them royally,
Their twigs and leaves abound;
Or grow their grapes abundantly
For others to astound.

If easy, narrow life they try
They'll weaken, wither, die.
If luscious fruitlessness is learned,
As useless they'll be burned.
If painful pruned and careful trained,
Great benefit for all is gained.

Driving in the Night

Driving in the night
I watched the road ahead
As far as headlamps' light –
Beyond that all is dead.

The ghostly trees and verge
Are all I see besides,
The shapes so faint they merge;
Behind them darkness hides.

In life my eyesight short
And blinkered vision keep
Me in the present caught –
No vision long or deep.
To find my way I must
In God's clear vision trust.

Climbing Above the Valley

People strolled the valley floor
Sipping beauty's easy savour,
Luscious trees and grass velour –
Of God's blessings just a flavour.

Some climbed high above the dale,
Straining up the stony wynd,
Reaching where they can unveil
Grander vistas to the mind.

Many are content to spend
Life in gentle, easy days;
Some will strive, their hearts extend
From time to time their views and ways;
Few with then expend their might
Raising soul to soaring height.

The Path

My path began in meadows broad
So clearly marked and trod with ease,
Then climbed the hillside's gentle sward
Across a stream and entering trees.

The steepening path, though clear before,
Now crossed with roots, cascades and rocks,
It bucked and twisted, turned and tore
'Cross outcrops, bogs my pathway blocked.

The markings failed, the maps obscure:
I guessed and tried, and missed my way,
With frequent halts to reassure
My place, and where my route now lay.

Despite wrong turns and misread maps,
Through all the marsh and tough terrain,
Despite all errors and mishaps,
Yet found I life's eventual aim.

The Turning

He wondered wistfully around the wreathen wynd,
Wandering in mystery the pathways of his mind,
Reflecting wretchedly on meaning and on cause,
His own short history the only thing assured.

He saw so shamefully how dire his kinsmen's plight,
How man grasps greedily his fellow's joy cup light,
And while he painfully sips at this poisoned cure
He mocks the misery his victim must endure.

As roamed he far and wide within his thoughts alone
He looked his soul inside and found that to his shame
A draught of others' cheer stood bitter there within:
It shook him through with fear that he these sins had known.
His anguished soul cried long, and from his spirit came
Resolve to right this wrong, and freedom's joys to win.

The Cloud

I walked beneath a cloud
So thund'rous, threatening, grey
As once, naïve and proud
My future 'fore me lay:
Potential joys and fears,
Success, mistakes and tears.

I walked on through the cloud
Forlorn, meandering, lost
As frequent setbacks shroud
My ways at awful cost.
Life stumbled left and right
My thwarted paths to blight.

I climbed above the cloud,
Its sumptuous beauty bright
As memories all crowd
And build in brave hindsight
My character, career,
My wisdom, skills and cheer.

A Different Beauty

I went there a beauty to seek,
Refreshing my soul and my heart
And purge from a difficult week
The stress of my life a large part.

By different byways I strayed,
A different beauty I found –
A different heartstring it played,
A tune with another fair sound.

Now beauties diverse do I find,
From each a new chord receives speech,
All dancing in soul now I find
My heartstrings great harmonies teach.
Now symphonies play in my mind
By heartstrings that heaven can reach.

A Droughted Tree

A droughted tree may freely choose
To spread its boughs and roots, and use
Its efforts hoping for swift rain
To fast imbibe, its strength regain.
Yet should relentless sun and sky
Delay their blessings, it would die.

A wiser tree withdraws its growth
And sheds its leaves in seeming sloth,
Appearing dead above the ground,
Its burrowing roots e'er deeper found
Some sips of moisture here and there,
Sustaining life through seasons bare.

When rain returns, exuberantly
Then some trees sprout luxuriantly,
Enjoying ease and beauty's signs,
Preparing not for sterner times
While mocking those who persevere
In growing strength for times severe.

The wiser tree the stronger grows
For all of life's travails and woes.
Our lives have frequent storm and drought
That help us grow resilient, stout,
Well strengthened by adversity
For glory through eternity.

Ways

So hard I've searched my way to find,
My purpose and my peace of mind,
My calling and my higher goal,
Fulfilment for my heart and soul.

For some it seems well marked and wide,
Though many dangers always hide
With tricks to spring we can't foresee
And question our integrity.

For others hard to see, unsigned,
Yet clear when found, and well defined,
While arduous in rock and hill
To challenge always heart and will.

For others always hid, unmarked
Through trackless jungle, moorland stark,
Cross oceans wide or mountains high,
Their hearts to follow, not their eye.

So each unique must seek their way,
Determined follow, night and day,
To find their own true destiny
Their hearts to fill, their souls to free.

Wait and See

He's gone. Again. And yet, and yet…
He said he's always there
With all who love and don't forget
To follow everywhere.

Wait here, he said, as rose he high;
I'm present though unseen.
Just as he'd said he'd die and rise –
Impossible to dream.

The Holy Spirit comes before –
His riddles leave us blind;
Yet showed he that the blind see more
Than sighted elders find.
A transformation mystery?
I think I'll wait and see.

Love Unshrouded

What beauty lies in love unshrouded,
Raw and un-reserved?
What joy in giving, self unclouded,
Free and undeserved?

What works achieved by love unshirking,
Each their burden share?
What wonders built from joyful working
With unstinting care?

What peace would flow from love unthreatening,
Tolerant and kind?
What harmony from such love beckoning,
Sharing heart and mind?

Such nature is the Trinity,
One and all divine,
Three persons joined in unity,
Love and joy sublime.

What wonder to be asked to share
Love and life so pure,
In Father, Son and Spirit's care
Ever to endure!

What world could we together build
Should such love we give?
And how our yearning hearts be stilled
Should such life we live?

The New Refrain

Take the embers of my heart,
The sole remains of love so strong,
Consumed by singing in the song
Of harmonies now torn apart.

Take the wreckage of my will
Which sailed, once master of the seas,
Now blown by every passing breeze;
Though dashed on rocks the hulk floats still.

Light my heart's fast cooling coals,
To warm once more the melody;
Abate the siren songs for me,
Re-float the wreckage from the shoals.
Be my compass, sails and stays,
Be my words, my tune, my praise.

Evolution of Prayer

Lord, I want to have.
Lord, I want for me.
Lord, I want to save.
Lord, I want to be.

Lord, please grant for us.
Lord, please keep us safe.
Lord, please help us trust.
Lord, your burdens chafe.

Lord, please help us do.
Lord, please let us know.
Lord, please help us through.
Lord, which way to go?

Lord, what is your will?
Lord, which is your way?
Lord, keep with us still.
Lord, what would you say?

Thank you for this gift.
Thank you for that prayer.
Thank you for life's lift.
Thanks for being there.

Praise for all you are.
Praise for all you do.
Praise for all your care.
Lord, I love you true.

Love Rejoices

The world, its mountains, lakes and trees,
All creatures in the air and earth,
The vast blue skies and teeming seas,
'Twas love unbounded brought to birth.

Mankind and angels, free to choose,
To think, to work, do good or ill,
To love and win, to turn and lose,
The summit of love's bounteous will.

All nature's laws that rule the world,
Sustaining, checking, pouring more;
The moral order long unfurled,
All drawn from love's unfathomed store.

Rejection, hatred, greed and spite,
Offending love and seeking ill,
The venom flooding 'gainst all right –
Yet love endures and keeps us still.

Derided, scorned, thrown out as dross,
Rejected, parodied, beset,
Scourged and mocked, nailed to a cross –
And love outreaching seeks us yet.

Inspiring goodness in a few,
His seeds of love embraced and fed,
Allowed to comfort, heal, renew –
So love's eternal joy is wed.